HELPING LEADERS TAKE EFFECTIVE ACTION

A Program Evaluation

HELPING LEADERS TAKE EFFECTIVE ACTION
A Program Evaluation

Dianne P. Young
Nancy M. Dixon

Center for Creative Leadership
Greensboro, North Carolina

The Center for Creative Leadership is an international, nonprofit educational institution founded in 1970 to foster leadership and effective management for the good of society overall. As a part of this mission, it publishes books and reports that aim to contribute to a general process of inquiry and understanding in which ideas related to leadership are raised, exchanged, and evaluated. The ideas presented in its publications are those of the author or authors.

The Center thanks you for supporting its work through the purchase of this volume. If you have comments, suggestions, or questions about any Center publication, please contact Walter W. Tornow, Vice President, Research and Publication, at the address given below.

Center for Creative Leadership
Post Office Box 26300
Greensboro, North Carolina 27438-6300

CENTER FOR CREATIVE LEADERSHIP

©1996 Center for Creative Leadership

CCL No. 174

Library of Congress Cataloging-in-Publication Data

Young, Dianne P.
    Helping leaders take effective action : a program evaluation / Dianne P. Young, Nancy M. Dixon.
        p.   cm.
    Includes bibliographical references.
    ISBN 1-882197-18-6
    1. Leadership. 2. Leadership—Study and teaching. 3. Executives—Training of. I. Dixon, Nancy M., 1937- . II. Title.
HD57.7.Y68 1996
658.4'071244—dc20
                                                          96-5307
                                                              CIP

Table of Contents

List of Tables and Figures

Executive Guide

In 1991 CCL's LeaderLab® program was launched with the goal of helping executives take more effective action in their leadership situations. Conducted over a period of six months, the program includes traditional and nontraditional features that encourage participants to become aware of management behaviors that need change, support them in making those changes, and assist them in devising and implementing action plans. Recently, an evaluation was conducted to see if the program was meeting its goal. This report discusses an important part of that evaluation.

Methodology

An *Impact Questionnaire,* developed by researchers for the study, was administered to the co-workers of LeaderLab participants to measure effectiveness before and after the program. Also, telephone interviews were conducted with participants, their co-workers, and their process advisors (CCL staff members who guide participants through the program); questions were asked about the nature of the participants' action plans and their progress in implementing them. A second set of telephone interviews, with participants only, asked if the program features specifically designed to support action-taking (for example, keeping a journal and visioning) were successful.

Findings

The *Impact Questionnaire* revealed that participants were perceived as having made significant positive change on every category except Balance (for example, in Self-assessment, in Listening, in Subordinate Development) and that this positive change is associated with increased effectiveness. The first set of telephone interviews revealed that participants took the most action in the following areas: Interpersonal Relationships, Organizational Systems, Coping with Emotional Disequilibrium, Facilitating Communication/Listening, Sense of Purpose/Vision, and Balance/Family. The second set of telephone interviews showed that among the action-oriented features, participants favored the assistance of the process advisor, the program's structure, the visioning and action-planning exercises, the diversity of participants, and the artistic activities. (See pages xi and xii for a summary of the findings.)

There were also some unanticipated results. Researchers found that many, if not most, of the participants came to the program with a reasonable amount of turbulence in their personal and work lives. They reported four types of turbulence that affected their carrying out of their action plans: general work-related (for example, downsizing or a new CEO); job specific (for example, promotion or a new job); personal (for example, an ill spouse or separated from spouse); and psychological (for example, depression and alcoholism).

A second unanticipated result was that in addition to finding out what action plans participants pursued, information was obtained on how they approached their action planning. They approached implementation from three different models: *goal focus,* whereby the participant set a goal for action and stuck to it, not going beyond it; *vision focus,* whereby the partici-pant viewed the action plan as merely a step in a process of working toward a larger vision; and *process focus,* whereby the participant viewed the action planning as an ongoing process used to conduct work and communicate with others.

Conclusions and Implications

The findings clearly suggest that this long-term, action-focused pro-gram can be helpful to executives who want to improve their leadership effectiveness.

This evaluation has implications for both practitioners and researchers. It is relevant to three groups of practitioners: program designers, program participants, and program evaluators. It says to program designers that en-couragement to take action in a supportive environment is a useful approach for developing executives.

It says to potential participants who are considering action-focused programs that they should be strongly committed to making changes, taking action, and monitoring their development over time. If they are in unstable situations or experiencing considerable turbulence, distractions, or lack of back-home support, it says that it is an important factor to consider.

To program evaluators it says that both quantitative and qualitative methods must be used to most efficiently assess an action-oriented program. If the skills to use both methods are not available, it is worthwhile for evalua-tors (as well as program designers and trainers) to form partnerships to gain the necessary expertise.

To researchers, the evaluation says that the relationship between the amount of turbulence in participants' lives and the actions they take warrants further study. Also, the three approaches to action planning (goal-, vision-, and process-focused) may be a starting point for looking at alternative ways to conceptualize and implement action plans.

Summary of Data Collection and Results
(all data collected after the program)

ACTION-TAKING OUTCOME MEASURES

Is LeaderLab Meeting Its Goal of Participants Taking More Effective Action in Their Leadership Situation?

Method 1:   *Impact Questionnaire* (14 scales, 92 items)

Measures changes in individual that led to action.
Asks raters to describe according to the 92 items:
– the person one year ago,
– the person now,
– and if a difference in the two, indicate the impact of change on the person's effectiveness.

Sample: 29 people who had completed program
38 people who had not yet attended program (control group)

Highlights of Results: The group that completed the program was perceived as having made significant positive change in every category except Balance.
– The greatest change was on Self-assessment.
– The smallest change was on Balance.

If participants got higher ratings now versus a year ago on a particular item, they were seen as being more effective.

Note: The control group made fewer changes than the study participants.

Method 2:   *First set of telephone interviews*

Focused on the implementation of action plans back on the job based on the written action plan prepared during the second week of training at CCL; also asked exploratory questions regarding the action-planning process.

Answers content-analyzed into 20 action categories (plus one category of miscellaneous)—see Table 6.

Sample: 27 study participants, their co-workers, and process advisors

Highlights of Results: Half of the reported actions (excluding miscellaneous) are represented by the following categories: Interpersonal Relationships, Organizational Systems, Coping with Emotional Disequilibrium, Sense of Purpose/Vision, Balance/Family, and Communication/Listening.

(continued)

Summary of Data Collection and Results (continued)
(all data collected after the program)

ACTION-ORIENTED DESIGN FEATURES AND METHODS

Method 3:   *Second set of telephone interviews*

Asked how a specific method or design feature had helped participants take more effective action.

Sample: 32 study participants

Highlights The top five major contributors to program outcomes in rank
of Results: order are: process advisor, program structure, visioning and action planning, diversity of participant group, and artistic activities.

Acknowledgments

Throughout this project we have been supported by a number of individuals who made significant contributions to our thinking, research, and finally, the writing of this report. First, our heartfelt thanks to the LeaderLab Advisory Group for their energy, ideas, advice, and support: Bob Burnside, Nur Gryskiewicz, Cindy McCauley, Chuck Palus, and Ellen Van Velsor. And without Victoria Guthrie's continuing support as Program Manager we would never have survived the data collection, nor seen the results of our work enrich LeaderLab. Also, we couldn't have done any of this without the support of the LeaderLab staff, who taught us about the program and accommodated our research needs into a very tightly woven program. Many thanks also to John Fleenor for his patience and wisdom in advising us on statistical issues.

We thank the Writer's Advisory Group for excellent feedback on early drafts of the report—Bob Burnside, Cheryl De Ciantis, Bill Drath, Cindy McCauley, Marian Ruderman, Ellen Van Velsor, and Martin Wilcox. The external reviewers—Tim Baldwin, John Hattie, Claire Muhm, and Ray Noe—supplied immeasurable help with their suggestions for improvements. To Edna Parrott and Lee Stine, we thank you for taking charge of the many administrative details, and to Marcia Horowitz thanks for making this report a reality through your editing expertise. Finally, we acknowledge the contributions of those LeaderLab pioneers who gave their own time, energy, and spirit to this research. This report is dedicated to them.

Introduction

Learning about one's strengths and weaknesses is an important aspect of leadership development. Executives, however, also need to practice learning through taking action. In 1991 CCL launched a program called LeaderLab®, which aims to help individuals take effective and sustained action in their leadership situations. Action is defined here as the translation of self-knowledge into specific activities that can help enhance leadership capabilities. LeaderLab participants are helped to do this through developing an action plan, and they are supported in this effort by both traditional (360-degree feedback and classroom work) and action-oriented (visioning, journaling, acting exercises) program features.

In order to determine if the program meets the goal of helping individuals take effective action, CCL researchers conducted an evaluation that provided information on the impact of the program on leadership effectiveness and the contribution of the program's special action-oriented design features to that impact. This report presents and discusses the major parts of the study. (Additional information about this evaluation can be found in Young, 1993; Young & Hefferan, 1994.)

We begin with a brief description of LeaderLab and then discuss how the program was evaluated. We will next present our findings and discuss them and then consider the nonprogram factors that may have affected these findings. Finally, we will address the implications for practice and research.

Description of LeaderLab

Through 1995, open-enrollment LeaderLab programs had run over 30 times and well over 500 participants had attended. The program expands on CCL's traditional model of a development program, which focuses on self-awareness. The main difference is that LeaderLab provides mechanisms for support and accountability over an extended period of time (six months) to help participants take action back in the workplace.

Figure 1 shows the basic structure of the program and the processes that take place during its separate phases.

Structure

LeaderLab is a six-month program, with two separate weeks of classroom activity, each followed by three months during which action plans are implemented. Mid- and upper-level managers from a variety of organizations

Figure 1
LeaderLab® Design

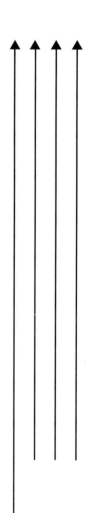

Apply to
Program

Acceptance

Prework and
Process Advisor
Phone Call
(6 weeks prior)

Attend Week 1
Training (6 days)
Develop Action
Plan

3 Months
Back on Job

Attend Week 2
Training
(3-1/2 days)
Revise Action Plan

2-1/2 Months
Back on Job

Complete
Program (Essay,
last PA Contact)

Ongoing Processes:
Process Advisor
Learning Journal
Vision and Action Plans
Change Partners

are selected in order to produce diversity in the participant group. Prior to the program, participants complete numerous self-assessments, have co-workers evaluate their performance, and do an audit of their current work situation. Each participant is contacted before the program starts by a *process advisor* (PA), who will serve as his or her personal coach over the next six months.

The program begins with six days at CCL. Participants receive feedback on their assessments and co-worker evaluations, meet with their PAs, learn from lectures and discussions, and engage in a number of experiential and nontraditional learning activities. They develop relationships with what are called *change partners* within the participant group, who provide support and with whom they process what they are learning.

Developing an action plan is key to the program and the process takes participants through several steps, ranging from guided visualization to the development of an actual written plan for action. This plan typically includes several statements that prescribe taking specific actions, such as focusing on the needs of external and internal customers or focusing on achieving balance in work and personal life. As part of the plan the participant is asked to provide concrete short- and long-term goals toward attaining success through taking the actions.

After their initial six days, the participant returns to work for three months and implements his or her action plan. Each keeps a learning journal, which is used for reflection and for communication with the PA, and establishes a second set of change partners in their back-home environment, who provide support and feedback for the actions they are working on. PAs contact participants by phone at least once each month to support and challenge their efforts to become more effective.

Three months later, the participants return to CCL for four days to process their learning and again participate in various classroom activities. They spend time with the PA and revise their action plans, taking into account what has been learned in the first three months. After the second session, participants work to implement their revised plans during the two-and-a-half remaining months of the program. They continue to engage in journal writing, interact with their back-home change partners, and talk with their PAs as a way to reflect on their actions and garner support.

The program ends after six months, at which time the participant provides an in-depth written summary of the experience and has a final conversation with the PA. An annual network meeting of all program alumni is held to provide continued support and learning.

Content

There are three areas of content in the program: (1) challenges faced by leaders going into the next century; (2) competencies to deal with the challenges; and (3) skills and knowledge for self-development (Burnside & Guthrie, 1992).

The challenges include dealing with rapid and substantive change; managing diversity of people and views; building the future through a shared sense of purpose; and dealing with each individual's leadership situation.

Five competencies address these challenges. Although distinct in focus, there is some overlap among the competencies because they were designed to be integrative: dealing effectively with *Interpersonal Relationships*; thinking and behaving in terms of *Organizational Systems*; approaching decision making from the standpoint of *Trade-offs*; thinking and acting with *Flexibility*; and maintaining emotional balance by *Coping with Emotional Disequilibrium*.

There are two major aspects of self-development that foster the skills and knowledge needed to both understand the leadership situation and to take action: learning from experience and clarifying the individual's sense of purpose. Briefly, learning from experience requires two methods: going-against-the-grain activities and structured reflection. Going against the grain (GAG) refers to the idea that learning can be facilitated by situations that are personally difficult or uncomfortable (Bunker & Webb, 1992). Structured reflection is built into the program through a daily learning journal which helps the participant probe specific events for reactions, behaviors, and so forth.

Sense of purpose is rooted in the idea that people need strong motivation to take action. This motivation can develop out of an increased awareness of an ideal or vision for the future and a clear picture of the needs of the current leadership situation. During the first week the program works with the individual leader's sense of purpose; during the second week it focuses more on developing a shared sense of purpose with the workgroup or organization, referred to as "building the future."

For a complete discussion of these content areas, see Burnside and Guthrie (1992).

Action-oriented Features

Several features were created for LeaderLab that are meant to help the participant create and sustain an effective plan for action. They are used in concert with more conventional training methods. Table 1 summarizes the action-oriented features and their rationales.

Table 1
Action-oriented Features and Their Rationales

Technique	*Rationale*

Action Learning Over Time
  Multiple training sessions
  Implementation of action
    plans
	Facilitates learning over time, which leads to change; addresses real issues, which helps transfer learning to leadership situation.

Developmental Relationships
  Process advisor
  Change partners
	Encourages learning through others (support for change—feedback—challenges—wisdom/advice) as a lifelong strategy for development.

Reflective Learning Journal	Connects participant to program over six months, which helps distill patterns, identify key lessons, encourage self-analysis. Provides content for process advisor phone calls.
Visioning and Action Planning	Provides process and structure for targeting changes and improvements—emphasizing the positive or "ideals" to guide change process.

Nontraditional Activities
  Acting
  Artistic work
  3-D problem solving
	Taps creative, emotional sides of learning by helping get outside the box of linear thinking. Also emphasizes importance of using affective and behavioral domains as well as cognitive.

Action learning over time. One of the aims of the program is to connect learning, over time, to the back-home leadership situation. LeaderLab attempts to make this happen through two training sessions, the implementation of action plans back in the workplace, and the continuous work with the PA and change partners. This closely parallels a process termed *action learning* (Argyris, Putnam, & Smith, 1985; Dixon, 1994; Revans, 1983), which posits real-world action as a valuable source of knowledge about self and, conversely, views organizational change as a manifestation of individual growth and development. LeaderLab embraces the fundamentals of action learning: The problems participants address are real; they deal with them over time and with the support and confrontation of their change partners and PA; and in the process they change both themselves and the system in which they function.

Developmental relationships. Learning through others can be a potent developmental experience (Bunker & Webb, 1992; Kram, 1988; McCall, Lombardo, & Morrison, 1988; McCauley & Hughes-James, 1994; McCauley & Young, 1993; Morrison, 1992). LeaderLab uses developmental relationships in two ways. First, the PA helps tailor the program to the individual needs of the participant. PAs play a variety of roles: expert, dialogue partner, accountant, encourager, feedback provider, and counselor. These roles are more fully described in McCauley and Young (1993) and Young and Hefferan (1994).

Second, participants are grouped into triads during the first week of training so that they can practice involving others in their leadership improvement process (Burnside & Guthrie, 1992). Called *change partners,* they continue to work together using each other as a resource throughout the program. Participants are also asked to set up a similar system back home. They are instructed to look for individuals who can give them support and encouragement, advice based on similar attempts at change, and honest feedback (Burnside & Guthrie, 1992).

Because many of the changes require personal change (such as being a more effective listener or handling conflict), participants sometimes ask a spouse or significant other to be a back-home change partner. All change-partner relationships are designed to provide follow-up and support as participants work on their action plans.

Reflective learning journals. Learning journals, which document events and record important issues, facilitate the contact between participant and PA during time away from class. Reports of the benefits of learning journals include enhancing reflective thinking skills; distilling lessons from experience; encouraging self-analysis that is independent of the classroom; and tracking learning, important lessons, trends, and patterns over time (Cell, 1984; McCauley & Hughes-James, 1994; Petranek, Corey, & Black, 1992; Wills, 1994; Young & Hefferan, 1994). The journals, which are routinely sent to the PA and provide much of the content during the phone conversations, are personal and confidential. No one but the PA ever sees it unless the participant chooses to share it with another staff member.

Visioning and action-planning process. Each participant spends part of the first training week clarifying his or her individual sense of purpose, vision, and action plan. The visioning process consists of guided visualizations to help the participant get a picture of their ideal leadership situation. The action-planning process consists of multiple attempts to articulate the vision and then determine the steps needed to work toward the vision. Participants are asked to take action at three levels: personal, group, and systems. The steps should be doable over the following three months.

The second training week emphasizes the same processes but with a different focus. Each participant is asked to develop a beginning vision and action plan for the group he or she has leadership responsibility for—as a basis for the development of a shared sense of purpose. Participants are then encouraged to work with their groups after the second training week to further develop the shared sense of purpose and vision. Again, the action steps should be doable over the following three months. Visioning and action planning focus on learning through implementation.

Expectations are that learning from reflecting on the actions taken will shape the vision and that the vision will shape the actions taken. Thus, it is an iterative and dynamic process.

Nontraditional activities. LeaderLab has incorporated several nontraditional classroom activities including acting, artistic work, and three-dimensional (3-D) problem solving. The intent of these is to help participants better understand leading "as a performing art" (Vaill, 1989). In his book *Artful Work*, Dick Richards (1995) writes, "While all work can be artful, leadership absolutely requires artfulness in a way that other work does not, because leadership involves vision and human energy" (p. 105). Cheryl De Ciantis (1995), a trainer who conducts one of the artistic activities, further states, "I learned the value of providing ways for people to temporarily get 'outside the box' of their accustomed mode of organizing experience, by taking a detour around the verbal, usually linear, logical structures which can harden into set habits of thinking" (p. xii). These activities can be controversial—perceived as uncomfortable and disconnected from the program and therefore a "GAG" (going against the grain) experience for some participants. However, they can also provide powerful learning experiences for many.

How the Program Was Evaluated

Although LeaderLab incorporates traditional methods such as lectures and 360-degree feedback, we chose to examine the features most directly related to action taking.

The Sample

Fifty-one executives who attended one of three LeaderLab runs between March 1992 and February 1993 participated in the evaluation. Of these, two were dropped because they were CCL staff members; one person did not complete the program; and 11 did not participate in any of the data collection. Thirty-seven participants completed some part of the data collection. Therefore, our data analysis is based on subgroups of the 37 and varies according to the research question addressed. The group of 37 was primarily male (77%) and white (89%) with an average age of 43 (range 32-55). Over half (57%) of the group had a master's or doctor's degree and tended to hold positions relatively high in the organizational hierarchy (46% upper-middle managers; 27% executive level; and 13.5% CEO level). The largest percentage (57%) were employed by private businesses, and 16% worked in either education or government.

How do the individuals in this sample compare to all of the others who have participated in the program since its inception? Based on 563 participants in LeaderLab (excluding those in this study), the larger pool was primarily male (65%) and white (85%) with an average age of 43 (range 28-61). Like our sample, this group tended to acquire advanced degrees, with 66% holding either a master's or doctor's degree. They too held positions relatively high in the hierarchy (37% upper-middle managers; 34% executive level; and 10% CEO level). A much larger percentage were employed in private businesses (76%). Overall, the profiles of the two groups are similar, indicating that the evaluation group should be representative of the larger LeaderLab population.

Data Collection

To find out if the program helped participants become more effective, we collected data in three ways: first by measuring the change in the individual that led to him or her taking action (the *Impact Questionnaire*); second, by gathering information on the ways individuals took action (first set of telephone interviews) and then comparing the respective quantitative and qualitative data; and third, by evaluating the several action-oriented program features in terms of how they contributed to effective action taking (second set of telephone interviews).

The *Impact Questionnaire*. The quantitative outcome measure was the *Impact Questionnaire*, developed specifically for this study. It employs a retrospective methodology, which assesses perceptions of change directly rather than attempting to infer change from ratings collected before and after the program. (For further details about methodology, see the Appendix, pages 40-42.)

We developed the questionnaire by collecting open-ended data from program alumni and their raters that related to changes the participants made during the program. The data were content-analyzed independently by two researchers and the results were used to develop broad categories of change. Items were written for the categories and piloted with program alumni. Revisions were made to the items and categories based on the results.

The questionnaire contains 92 items, which are clustered into 14 categories. These categories are then divided into *Competencies* and *Other*. The competencies represent the skills that effectively address the LeaderLab challenges (see page 4). Table 2 gives a short description of each category with a sample item. (See Table A1 for their alphas.)

The questionnaire, administered after program completion, asks participants and their raters (co-workers) to respond to the 92 items in three ways[1]: (1) Circle the number that best describes the person one year ago (*Year Ago* rating); (2) Circle the number that best describes the person today (*Now* rating); (3) If there is a difference in the two ratings, indicate the impact of the change on the person's effectiveness (*Impact on Effectiveness* rating). (See Figure 2 for samples of items with the rating scales.)

All raters were guaranteed confidentiality and no feedback results were given to the participants (this was clearly pointed out beforehand). Both participants and their raters returned the questionnaires directly to us. We had 29 participants with usable data.

We also administered the *Impact Questionnaire* to a matched sample control group which consisted of individuals who had been accepted into the program but had not yet attended (*N*=38). By comparing the change scores of the two groups, we determined whether those who completed the program were perceived as making significantly more change than the control group.

First set of telephone interviews. The qualitative measure for gathering action-planning data was a set of telephone interviews conducted with 27 participants, their co-workers, and PAs, three to four months after completion of LeaderLab. The interview questions probed participants about how they approached the implementation of the action plans that were refined during the second week of the program. Exploratory questions were also asked about the action-planning process (see Table 3).

The types of actions/outcomes reported in the interviews were content-analyzed. We first made a master list of all actions/outcomes reported when at least *two* of the sources mentioned it. Then we developed categories of the actions and coded the master list of actions/outcomes into one of the categories, again divided by the two major groupings of *Competencies* and *Other*. This content analysis was not based on the *Impact Questionnaire* categories, although there is some overlap. (The Appendix contains the category names and a brief description of each on pages 38 and 39.)

Table 2
Impact Questionnaire Categories

COMPETENCIES

Coping with Emotional Disequilibrium: Coping with stress; remaining poised or calm during stressful events; is able to take action despite emotions.
> *Sample item:* Takes time to gain his/her composure before reacting to a personal attack.

Interpersonal Relationships: Interacting with others.
> *Sample item:* Shows sensitivity to how others are feeling.

Flexibility: Adaptability; openness to change; making changes as needed.
> *Sample item:* Adapts to new situations readily.

Organizational Systems: Focusing on the big picture; strategic; how I or my group fit into the big picture. Also understanding what it takes to make things happen within the system.
> *Sample item:* When trying to effect change, accounts for how it will fit into the big picture, impact the organization.

Trade-offs: Making decisions by weighing needs/goals of multiple stakeholders.
> *Sample item:* Attempts to maximize benefits for all parties involved when making a decision.

OTHER

Balance: Skills at balancing work and personal life.
> *Sample item:* Works evenings and weekends on a regular basis.

Climate: Interaction with the psychological (not physical) working environment.
> *Sample item:* Creates a relaxed climate at work.

Facilitating Communication: Setting up methods or creating new forms for facilitating communication.
> *Sample item:* Seeks ways to facilitate communication among staff.

Listening: Giving thoughtful attention to the information communicated by others.
> *Sample item:* Checks to be sure he/she understands the other person's message.

Seeking Feedback: Asking for/giving feedback; taking action based on the feedback.
> *Sample item:* Reacts defensively to suggestions on how he/she can improve his/her leadership style.

Self-assessment: Having awareness and doing ongoing evaluation of strengths, developmental needs, and impact on others.
> *Sample item:* Understands his/her strengths and weaknesses.

Self-confidence: Exhibiting changes that reflect self-assurance and a positive self-regard.
> *Sample item:* Believes he/she makes valuable contributions to the organization.

Sense of Purpose: Knowing and articulating what matters or is important to self; is willing to subordinate personal goals for shared group/organizational goals.
> *Sample item:* Makes it clear to others where he/she stands on an issue.

Subordinate Development: Creating opportunities for and/or placing emphasis on subordinates' growth and development.
> *Sample item:* Delegates exciting work to staff.

Figure 2
Impact Questionnaire Sample

Item	One Year Ago									Now									Impact on Effectiveness		
Understands his or her strengths and weaknesses	1	2	3	4	5	6	7	8	9	1	2	3	4	5	6	7	8	9	L	N	M
Takes time to gain his or her composure before reacting to a personal attack	1	2	3	4	5	6	7	8	9	1	2	3	4	5	6	7	8	9	L	N	M
Adopts a bullying style under stress	1	2	3	4	5	6	7	8	9	1	2	3	4	5	6	7	8	9	L	N	M
Shows sensitivity to how others are feeling	1	2	3	4	5	6	7	8	9	1	2	3	4	5	6	7	8	9	L	N	M

Key:
1 = Not at all
3 = To a small extent
5 = To a moderate extent
7 = To a great extent
9 = To a very large extent

Key:
L = Less effective
N = No impact on effectiveness
M = More effective

Table 3
Questions Used in First Set of Telephone Interviews

Selected Questions for Co-workers and Process Advisor

- What specific actions is (participant) currently taking to be more effective in his or her leadership situation?
- What enabled him or her to take these actions?
- (Refer to action plan) What progress did (participant) make on his or her action plan? (Read each action) What evidence do you have of this progress?

Selected Questions for Process Advisor

- Was there any evidence that the action plan changed over time? If so, what do you think caused the change?
- What other progress did you observe the participant making over the course of the program? What evidence did you have of this progress?

Selected Questions for Participant

- In the program you committed to a set of actions. What have you accomplished with respect to these actions?
- What specific actions are you taking now to be more effective in your leadership situation on a personal, group, and systems level?
- Has your action plan changed over time, and if so, what caused it to change?

Second set of telephone interviews. A qualitative measure was used to collect data about design features. In a second set of telephone interviews three to five months after the program, 32 participants were asked two questions about several of the action-oriented design features, such as PAs, visioning, and change partners: (1) Was the (design feature) helpful in enabling you to take more effective action? If so, how? (2) On a 1-to-10 scale, how would you rate (design feature) in terms of its helping you reach your goals?

The responses to the first question for each method or feature were content-analyzed. The participants' quantitative ratings were averaged, and the program methods and design features were ranked in descending order.

In addition, what we regard as a contextual factor, the diversity of the program group, was asked about because the population makeup is considered important to affecting outcomes.

Taking Action: Results and Discussion

Our question was: Is LeaderLab meeting its goal of helping participants take more effective action in their leadership situations? The results below are organized according to the method we used to gain the information. That is, we present the major findings of the *Impact Questionnaire* and the findings from the action-planning interviews to provide information on the kinds of changes participants made that led to action. We then describe the findings from the interviews that asked about design features and methods to show how these features contributed to participants' changes. Each is followed by a discussion. (For quick reference, highlights of the results are provided in the Executive Guide.)

What Kinds of Behavior Change Led to Action Taking (The *Impact Questionnaire*)?

The major findings from the *Impact Questionnaire* are:

(1) The program participants were perceived as having made significant positive change that led to taking effective action in every category except Balance. The improved means on all categories from *Year Ago* to *Now* in Table 4 show this improvement clearly. The greatest mean change was on Self-assessment and the smallest was on Balance.

(2) Overall, when participants got higher ratings now versus a year ago on a particular item, they were rated as more effective. (See the Appendix, pages 40-41.)

In support of the findings, a control group, consisting of people who had not yet taken the program, were found to have made fewer changes during the time period in question than the program participants.

Discussion. One explanation for the improvement in all categories (except Balance) may lie in the particular combination of action-oriented components in this program. For instance, the categories of Self-assessment and Seeking Feedback, which showed the highest mean change (Table 4), may have shown improvement because they are enhanced by various structures and processes. Participants receive a great deal of feedback via multi-rater questionnaires, change partners, and PAs. The learning journals are used in part to reflect on the feedback and what they are learning about themselves. The program also encourages participants to share their learnings about themselves with others, so it is not surprising that raters would be aware that participants were changing their views of themselves.

Also, in the second week of training LeaderLab emphasizes the participant's role in developing others, which may have led to the higher

Table 4
Change by Participants on *Impact Questionnaire* Categories
(N = 29)

| | Year Ago | | Now | | *Mean* |
	Mean	*Std.*	*Mean*	*Std.*	*Change*
Competencies:					
Flexibility	6.15	1.02	6.79	.86	0.63***
Organizational Systems	6.08	.98	6.70	.83	0.63***
Interpersonal Relationships	5.89	1.35	6.51	.92	0.62***
Coping with Emotional Disequilibrium	5.92	1.20	6.44	.91	0.52***
Trade-offs	5.84	.89	6.35	.75	0.51***
Other:					
Self-assessment	**5.33**	**1.00**	**6.13**	**.82**	**0.92*****
Seeking Feedback	5.41	.93	6.18	.77	0.77***
Climate	5.55	1.21	6.14	.86	0.59***
Facilitating Communication	5.71	.99	6.28	.98	0.57***
Subordinate Development	5.77	1.04	6.32	1.00	0.55***
Listening	6.00	1.12	6.50	.81	0.50***
Sense of Purpose	6.03	.78	6.35	.69	0.32***
Self-confidence	7.10	.70	7.31	.68	0.22*
Balance	**5.52**	**.62**	**5.72**	**1.07**	**0.20**

*p < .01
***p < .001

change scores on Subordinate Development. Listening, Facilitating Communication, and Climate are not specifically addressed in LeaderLab, yet they underlie much of the process. In addition, participants may improve here as a result of working on other things such as interpersonal relationships.

As to the finding on Balance (lowest mean change; Table 4), raters were not in a position to directly observe changes in this category. Balance had the largest standard deviation, indicating there was less agreement by raters on this category.

Self-confidence had the highest mean score for both *Year Ago* and *Now* ratings. This may be because the sample members occupied senior levels in the organization. We examined the self data as well to see if the trend of higher ratings held. It did; participants rated themselves highest on Self-confidence for both the *Year Ago* and the *Now* ratings. This may indicate that leadership development programs need not focus much attention on enhancing self-confidence, especially through 360-degree feedback.

The second major finding from the *Impact Questionnaire* concerns the analysis of impact on effectiveness. It is that overall, positive changes on the items (that is, higher *Now* ratings [Table 4]) are associated with increased effectiveness. This finding supports the idea that all of the categories measured are perceived as important and relevant to the leadership roles of LeaderLab participants. These findings, based on the mean change scores of raters, indicate strong impact in all categories except Balance.

Control-group comparisons. The comparison of participants who completed the program with the control group who hadn't yet participated was useful because the findings underscored that LeaderLab participants who completed the program were changing positively as a result and, thus, were taking more effective action. Table 5 shows that the participant group was seen as having changed significantly more than the control group: In eight out of fourteen categories (Coping with Emotional Disequilibrium, Interpersonal Relationships, Flexibility, Organizational Systems, Trade-offs, Self-assessment, Subordinate Development, and Listening), change was significantly greater for the participant group. According to the *t* values in the fourth column of Table 5, which indicate significance levels, the greatest differences were on Self-assessment, Organizational Systems, and Trade-offs.

The six categories where there was no significant difference between the two groups are: Seeking Feedback, Facilitating Communication, Climate, Balance, Sense of Purpose,[2] and Self-confidence.[3]

Most of the differences between the two groups were moderate (.4 to .5). (Effect size was used to indicate magnitude of difference; see Table A2.) This could mean LeaderLab is not maximizing impact or that the control group is already working on behaviors in most of the categories we measured, although to a lesser extent than the participants who completed the program.

In What Ways Did Participants Approach Implementation of Action Plans (First Set of Telephone Interviews)?

The first set of telephone interviews asked about the ways in which participants approached the action plans they revised during the second class session. The interview data were content-analyzed independently by two researchers into categories of actions. Some of these overlap with those on the *Impact Questionnaire*. There were twenty categories of actions reported, including a miscellaneous category comprised of items that were too situation-specific to code.

Table 5
Comparison of Mean Change Scores of Participant and Control Groups
on the *Impact Questionnaire*

Categories	Mean Change Group That Completed LeaderLab (N = 29)	Mean Change Control Group (N = 38)	t Value
Competencies:			
Flexibility	0.63***	0.34	3.09*
Organizational Systems	0.63***	0.35	3.19*
Interpersonal Relationships	0.62***	0.27	3.14**
Coping with Emotional Disequilibrium	0.52***	0.21	2.97*
Trade-offs	0.51***	0.25	3.92**
Other:			
Self-assessment	0.92***	0.44	3.35**
Seeking Feedback	0.77***	0.50	1.80
Climate	0.59***	0.28	2.17
Facilitating Communication	0.57***	0.35	1.81
Subordinate Development	0.55***	0.32	2.47*
Listening	0.50***	0.22	2.49*
Sense of Purpose	0.32***	0.21	1.39
Self-confidence	0.22*	0.08	1.87
Balance	0.20*	0.02	1.01

  $*p < .01$
 $**p < .001$
$***p < .0001$

Results. Table 6 depicts both the total number of actions reported by category (some participants had multiple actions reported in the same category) and number of participants with at least one reported action in the category. These results indicate that half of the reported actions (excluding the miscellaneous group) are represented by the following categories: Interpersonal Relationships, Organizational Systems, Coping with Emotional Disequilibrium, Sense of Purpose/Vision, Balance/Family, and Communication/Listening.

The categories that overlapped between the *Impact Questionnaire* data and the interview data are: Interpersonal Relationships, Organizational Systems, Communication/Listening, and Coping with Emotional Disequilibrium.

Discussion. The findings here are somewhat different from the *Impact Questionnaire* results in the following ways. There was not a significant

Table 6
Categories of Actions Taken
(*N* = 27)

Categories	Total # Actions Reported in the Category	# Participants Taking Action
Competencies:*		
Interpersonal Relationships	14	10
Organizational Systems	11	08
Coping with Emotional Disequilibrium	09	09
Other:		
Communication/Listening	16	14
Sense of Purpose/Vision	13	11
Balance/Family	12	10
Organizing the Job/Work	09	05
Openness	08	07
Subordinate Development	08	08
Utilizing LeaderLab Content or Processes	07	06
Self-awareness/Reflection	06	06
Self-confidence	06	05
Roles	06	04
Feedback	05	05
Health	05	04
Career	05	04
Climate	04	03
Perspective-taking	04	03
Getting Resources	03	03

Total = 151

Miscellaneous	20	16

*Flexibility and Trade-offs were not major themes in the data.

difference between the group that attended LeaderLab and the control group in the Balance category. Even so, Balance was an important category in terms of reported actions taken. As pointed out earlier, raters on the *Impact Questionnaire* were not in a position to observe changes in the Balance category. Sense of Purpose/Vision was also not a strong outcome based on the *Impact Questionnaire* data. Self-assessment, the category that showed the most change on the *Impact Questionnaire* data, was not found to be a strong program outcome in this analysis. Self-assessment was one of the content categories (called self-awareness/reflection), but, with only six reported actions, was a small category of impact.

The categories that overlapped—Interpersonal Relationships, Organizational Systems, Communication/Listening, and Coping with Emotional Disequilibrium—support the premise that LeaderLab is effectively using an action-learning approach. That is, participants are indeed changing both themselves and the systems in which they operate.

This leads us to the second set of telephone interviews, which probe some of the specific ways that the design features used in LeaderLab helped contribute to a positive outcome for participants.

How Did Action-oriented Design Features and Methods Contribute to Taking Action (Second Set of Telephone Interviews)?

In a second set of telephone interviews with program participants only, we asked how a specific method or design feature had helped them take more effective action; we did not ask if it led to a specific outcome or action. Table 7 displays the rank order on a 10-point scale of participant ratings of the program methods. They are discussed in that order.

Process advisors and program structure. The major contributors to program outcomes ranked first were: *process advisors (PAs)* and the *program structure* (stretching the intervention over six months through multiple sessions and an action-learning approach). These two features received the

Table 7
Participants' Rank Order of Ratings of Action-based Features
(*N* = 32)

Feature	Mean Rating
Process Advisor	8.9
Program Structure	8.2
Action Planning	7.8
Diversity of Participant Group	7.4
Artistic Activities	7.1
Acting	6.3
Journaling	6.3
Visioning	6.2
Change Partners	6.1
3-D Problem Solving	5.7

highest overall ratings on a 10-point scale as well as extremely favorable comments by participants.

The rank-order findings are consistent with results from earlier data collections around program effectiveness (Young & Burnside, 1993). However, our current findings are perhaps more meaningful than earlier results, because the data were collected three to four months after participants completed LeaderLab. We have found that ratings gradually decrease over time for most features (Young, 1993), so it is striking that these two features of the program continue to be perceived as key to program outcomes.

Every one of the 32 participants interviewed indicated that the PA had been helpful. The PAs are individuals with a variety of backgrounds, including clinical psychology, counseling, organizational change and development, career development and counseling, and management/leadership development. Participants reported that PAs did indeed play a variety of roles: expert, dialogue partner, accountant, positive reinforcer/encourager, feedback provider, and counselor. Participants made several remarks during their interviews that characterized these roles:

> My PA acted as a mirror for myself so I could see patterns, maintain consistency. The PA challenged me to explore my feelings and develop different strategies.

> The PA helped me visualize needed changes and showed me how to focus on the where and how in accomplishing my goal.

> The PA had no vested interest, so there was an impartial point of view. Helped me be clear on what was said around issues at work.

It should be noted that the expert role was almost always related to process, not content. The PAs did not give advice based on intimate knowledge of an industry or organization; rather they gave advice and suggested strategies based on their knowledge of change and development processes. The role of PA was intentionally *not* set up to be a content expert role but rather that of process expert.

Participants also told us that the PA's perceived objectivity and positive regard for them was a critical ingredient of successful relationships. Finally, we learned that the PAs provide both ongoing support and pressure for the participants as they work on their actions back home. This plays an important role in sustaining the participant's motivation, as one participant noted:

> The idea that you're going to have a person checking up on you from the beginning spurs you on. Having regular contact and support initiated by the process advisor was very helpful. Imposed a discipline.

As to the program structure, 31 of the 32 participants we interviewed in this part of the study thought that the program had the right flow, with the split training weeks and time for implementation of action plans back on the job spread over the six months. Returning to CCL for the second week of training was especially important in keeping participants motivated to work on their action plans and in helping them practice and integrate learnings from the first training week. Participant reactions were:

> I was dubious at first. Then everything clicked for me during week two at CCL. It was a revolutionary time for me. I realized the foundation must be laid in week two.

> Very effective plan for this coursework. The first session was a discovery process. The second allowed me to view what worked, what didn't, and why.

> If I hadn't known I was coming back, I would have run out of steam early on. I needed my batteries recharged and the energy the group gave me week two was critical.

Although we are not aware of any empirical studies comparing programs based on length or number of sessions, there is growing support for management and leadership development programs which have multiple sessions and which use an action-learning approach (Conger, 1992; Noe & Ford, 1992; Noel & Charan, 1989; Sadler, 1989; Wills, 1994).

Action planning. The most helpful aspect of action planning (part of the action-learning-over-time method) is the structure and organization it provides participants as they plan next steps toward achieving their vision back on the job. LeaderLab takes a somewhat different approach to this process than is typical in leadership development programs. The program assumes a process orientation toward action planning, meaning that participants are encouraged to draft a plan; work on implementation; reflect and distill learnings along the way; and revise, update, expand, or change the plan as needed. Thus, learning from actions taken over time and feeding that learning back into the action-planning process are critical. The point is not to get the perfect plan but rather to learn to use action planning as a lifelong tool for learning and increasing effectiveness.

Some participant comments on action planning are:

Helped me formalize steps needed to take concrete action. Allowed me to test progress—helped me develop a strategy.

Action planning creates investment in the program—commitment.

I learned how to break down my vision into smaller stages, so I could better understand where I was headed.

Diversity. In addition to questions about specific action-oriented program features, we also asked a demographic question about the influence of the program population on the participant. As we suspected, it came out in the top tier of scores in terms of its importance in achieving effectiveness. Although the program works to achieve diversity among the participant groups, our sample was primarily male and white. There was, however, diversity among job types and to a lesser degree among organization types. Twenty-eight of 32 participants found the diversity helpful, with most citing increased appreciation for and understanding of other perspectives as the greatest benefit. Other benefits mentioned included "bringing different issues to the table" and awareness that many problems are universal. Some partici- pants thought there should be more diversity among the group to include more international and mature participants.

Artistic activities. The artistic activities in the program are part of what are called *nontraditional training methods.* The artwork is facilitated by an artist and includes a drawing exercise, wherein participants are asked to depict their current leadership situation in terms of family, work, friends, interests and hobbies, and self-development; and a *touchstone exercise,* where participants construct a personally meaningful object out of natural materials. The touchstone provides an opportunity for participants to reflect on learn- ings, visions for change, and resulting action plans for improving leadership effectiveness. It provides a very personal way to express a metaphor or vision of change in a nonverbal way (De Ciantis, 1995). Because participants take the touchstone home with them after the first class week, it is a "living" reminder of the program and their commitment to change. It can also be used to communicate with others about the vision for change. Several participants mentioned that it added a fun or playful dimension to the program.

Journaling, visioning, and change partners. Although these ratings were modest, 25 participants stated that journaling was helpful primarily as a reflective learning tool. They used the journal to do such things as track patterns and trends; reflect back on actions to see what worked and what didn't; gain new perspectives and guide future actions; and deal with the emotional aspects of learning. Very few participants continued to journal after LeaderLab, citing discomfort with writing and the amount of time required, even though they found it valuable during the program. Participants expressed some frustration with not understanding the purpose of the journal earlier in the program.

Participants reported that visioning was primarily useful for narrowing and clarifying their ideas or for broadening and opening up their thinking. Reviews of this activity were mixed and included criticism of the guided-visualization technique. Responses concerning the back-home change partners were also mixed. When they were helpful to the participant they played roles similar to the PA, with feedback being especially important.

Successful relationships were characterized by the participant's being open in sharing and accepting feedback and the change partner's being perceived as trustworthy, discreet, committed, and available. These characteristics were lacking when participants indicated they did not find the change partners helpful.

Acting and three-dimensional problem solving. Like the artistic activities, acting and three-dimensional problem solving are also nontraditional training activities. "The Acting Leader" is conducted by a professional actor who works with participants to better understand and manage the impact of their physical presence. Three-D problem solving is facilitated by a person with special training in group work that involves the expression of emotion in nonverbal ways. Participants physically represent problems or issues by arranging, or sculpting, the group to demonstrate relationships, communication, and so forth. They then resculpt the group to represent the resolution of the problem. The activity is conducted silently, providing another avenue for nonverbal expression and learning.

There were no strong themes for how either of these methods were helpful. A few participants stated that acting class had physical benefits for handling stress, and some people reported increased awareness of the impact of voice and body language on others. The most frequent comments about the 3-D problem solving related to the emotional power of the activity. In fact, some participants criticized the use of this technique in the program because they were unprepared for the emotional impact. A number of participants also found this activity the most difficult to connect to the rest of LeaderLab.

Discussion. There are tensions involved in using such unconventional techniques in a program such as LeaderLab. These include risk and perceived relevance. Participants may feel foolish in doing the activities and need to be assured that their participation is voluntary. Also, each activity must be set up in a way that creates a safe environment for experimentation. Because the activities are stretching for many participants, it is important to address how they relate to leadership and the back-home situation. The activities need to be meaningfully embedded in the program, not at the end of each day, which might increase perceptions that they are not important or that they are "add ons." Debriefing the activities with the entire group is helpful so that participants learn from each other how the activities were useful or helpful. Finally, the demeanor of the staff is important. It must be clearly conveyed that the activities are core to the program.

There are also a number of benefits in using these types of activities. First, they provide an opportunity to practice learning through uncomfortable or stretching situations. Second, they can help disembed assumptions by externally representing them so that they can be examined. For example, a participant may discover through the touchstone that he or she has narrowly defined success and that a broader definition would be helpful. Finally, activities can help tap creativity, a benefit frequently commented upon by the participants.

Each of the action-based features contributed to program outcomes of participants taking more effective action. The degree of contribution varied, however. The PAs and program structure appear to work very well for almost every participant and, thus, overall contribute the most to program outcomes. Without the PAs and current program structure, the program outcomes would probably be very different. On the other hand, because of the variety of methods and design features used by LeaderLab, there is "something for everyone" regardless of preferred learning style.

Non-program Factors That Affected Participants' Taking Action

There are two additional issues that we looked into, although they were not studied as part of the major question we considered. First, the data revealed some unexpected results around how personal and work-related turbulence in participants' lives affected the action-planning process. Second, we wanted to look at how participants implemented their action plans.

The Effect of Turbulence on Action Planning

During LeaderLab, participants implemented their action plans within the context of a great deal of personal and work-related turbulence. We were surprised at the amount reported, particularly since we did not ask specifically about this in the interview protocol. It often came up as an explanation for why actions from the written plans had not been carried out or had taken an unanticipated direction. Had participants been asked about turbulence more directly, we may have seen even more of it reported.

Turbulence was reported for 19 out of the subsample of 27 participants. We have included illustrative comments in some cases, and it should be noted that the comments are drawn from both participant reports and others' (co-worker, PA) interviews. Thus, some quotes are clearly the participant describing a situation, and some comments obviously came from other sources.

We can operationally define turbulence as unanticipated occurrences that command the attention of the participant and are typically stressful. It was frequently, but not always, experienced negatively. The turbulence reported in this study can be grouped into four broad categories: system level, job specific, personal, and psychological (Table 8).

The four types of turbulence. System-level turbulence involved such events as downsizing, reorganization, and the replacement of senior management. Participants themselves appeared to have little impact on these occurrences, although they were greatly affected by them. Generally, participants in such situations focused on personal goals in their action plans rather than group or systemic goals. For example, three participants in this study were in organizations in which a profound cultural change occurred that was not congruent with the participants' goals and values. One of these changes resulted from a merger, the other two were situations in which a new CEO abruptly altered the organization's movement toward teamwork and participation. In all three cases the participants all but abandoned their group- and system-level goals in their action plans but did continue to make progress on their personal goals. Nine of the 27 participants had reports of some kind of system-level turbulence. Comments included: "His company merged with . . . , so two cultures merged. Values are not the same. He felt discontent due to this dilemma."

Occurrences in the job-specific category include taking a new job within the same organization, sometimes as a result of system-level changes; taking a job in a new organization; job loss, again often due to a systemic change; and moving between line and staff positions. Twelve participants had reports of this type of turbulence. One co-worker indicated, "We are downsizing. Within the last three weeks, he has been told that his position is being dissolved."

Occurrences in the personal category happened outside of the workplace, yet greatly affected how participants functioned at work. They included such events as personal health problems or those of family members; loss of a close relationship through separation or death; and the instigation of new relationships or resumption of a former one. Eight participants had reports of events in this category of personal turbulence. An example of the comments included: "He's in turmoil. He recently separated from his wife."

Occurrences in the psychological category tended to be long-standing problems such as alcoholism, depression, and chemical imbalances. In some cases the participant was learning to deal with the issue in a new way; in other cases he or she gained new insight into the impact of the problem on their work. Four participants had reports of turbulence in this area. One person stated, "The participant is also attending AA to help her overcome some of her problems."

The impact of turbulence. The turbulence manifested in these four categories clearly had an impact on participants' ability to carry out their

Table 8
The Four Categories of Turbulence: Participants' Responses
(N = 19)*

Work/ System Level	*Work/Job Specific*	*Personal*	*Psychological*
• Reorganization • Merge/Culture change/New boss • Reorganization • Downsizing • Partner left • Restructuring/ New CEO • New CEO/ Culture change • New CEO/ Culture change • Restructuring/ Downsizing	• New job—same organization • New job—new region • New job—line to staff • New job—same organization • New job— promotion • New job—line to staff • New roles—partner left • Promotion • Promotion • Promotion • New job—new organization • Lost job— downsizing	• Wife ill • Physical problems • Wife ill • Father's death • Reunited with wife and children • Separated from wife and children • Significant other moved in • Family counseling	• Depression • Alcoholism • Mood swings/ chemical imbalance • Emotional "roller coaster," mood swings
N = 9	*N = 12*	*N = 8*	*N = 4*

*Some participants reported multiple turbulent events.

action plans. However, the nature of that impact is less apparent in our data. In most cases the turbulence, even when it was negative, did not seem to prevent participants from making progress in some areas, although it did appear to influence which areas were focused on. It is unclear that it always fostered learning, although for some it seemed to do so. This preliminary finding is consistent with earlier LeaderLab research in which individuals who participated as case studies were found to have been more motivated when there was turbulence present in their lives. The program seemed to have greater impact on participants with a moderate amount of turbulence and pressure (Young, 1993).

Literature on stress and learning. Perhaps a look at a few of the relevant works on the relationship of stress and learning can help illuminate these findings. The most widely accepted model of stress is activation theory, based on Yerkes-Dodson's (1908) theory of arousal and performance. This model suggests a curvilinear relationship between stress and learning, with both low and very high stress resulting in little learning.

Bunker and Webb (1992) note that the stresses of work and nonwork life are interactive. They look for stress in what individuals avoid or ignore, in particular those situations that threaten self-image and exceed the individual's ability to respond.

Bandura (1977) identifies two potential outcomes from stressful situations: learning and avoidance. There are two powerful expectations that influence which outcome might occur: efficacy expectations (the belief that one is capable of doing what is required) and outcome expectations (the belief that a given behavior will lead to certain outcomes). In relation to the latter, for example, a manager might feel unable to affect the merger of his or her company and thus focus on coping with negative feelings rather than learning from the situation. In terms of efficacy expectations, an example might be a manager who felt unable or unprepared to take on the marketing responsibilities of the firm. In both cases, the negative assessment could result in avoidance rather than learning. Certainly efficacy and outcome expectations are heavily influenced by past experience. Avoidance behavior tends to be self-reinforcing by preventing the individual from discovering what might be new about a situation.

In our study avoidance behavior may have been reduced to some degree by the PA, one of whose tasks is to confront the participant with those behaviors which he or she might, in fact, be avoiding. In addition, the PA may have provided a positive influence on self-efficacy by expressing belief that the participant would be able to take on greater levels of responsibility. For example, many participants who were embroiled in turbulence talked about the PA as a "lifeline" or said that the PA "got me through it." Likewise the staff, other program participants, and back-home change partners may have increased learning by having a positive effect on both outcome and efficacy expectations. Others talked about the program occurring at "just the right time." It may well be that without the support the program provided, particularly through the PA, some of the learning that was gained from and through the turbulence would not have happened. McCauley and Hughes-James (1994, p. 50) also found that turbulence could be either a distraction from change efforts or that a development program could provide critical support to help the participant learn from difficult situations.

Ways in Which Participants Implement Action Plans

In the evaluation, we looked at how participants *approached* their action-planning tasks. In addition, we wanted to know how participants *implemented* action planning, so we asked several exploratory questions in our first set of telephone interviews. We found evidence in the interview data that participants approached implementation of action plans from three different models: goal focus, vision focus, and process focus.

Goal focus. The first model, goal focus, is reflective of the way action plans are most commonly referenced in the literature: goals to be attained. These participants answered the interview questions as though the action planning was a blueprint for specific actions, and the other interviewees indicated the participant held this view. In other words, they tended to take the action-planning process quite literally. Rarely were there reports of actions beyond the specific steps they committed to on paper in the program. Examples of comments included: "Didn't do anything outside of his action plan. He was very focused."

Vision focus. In the second model, vision focus, the participants seemed to view the items on the action plan as beginning steps for a more extensive plan. They regarded the individual items they had written into the action plan as a kind of tip-of-the-iceberg. The iceberg itself included the vision the participant had created during the program. Participants seemed to carry a mental image of an ideal state (vision) they were working toward, more than specific items written on the plan. Their actions often took advantage of, or responded to, opportunities that occurred in their environment. Thus, actions definitely changed, and in some cases the vision seemed to evolve as well. This model seemed to be the most prevalent among participants in this study. An example of a participant comment was: "But I believe that all visions change. A vision always starts vague and gets more focused as you start to work with what's available."

Process focus. The third model, process focus, means how one conducts work. These participants viewed action planning as an ongoing process that involves acting, reflecting, and revising actions. They tended to use their action plan as a way to communicate with others about what they were trying to accomplish or do differently. Some participants talked about using the action-planning process and, in some cases, the material from LeaderLab with their teams to work toward a shared vision. From this perspective, the initial steps written on paper were viewed as just an iteration of a process that would continually evolve. Thus, anything written on paper would be "old news" within a short period of time, given the dynamic and ever-changing environment these leaders were operating within. One participant stated, "Action planning is a waste of time but a paradox. I can't get out of doing it; no action plan stays constant, but without one you can't get anything done." This view of action planning was least prevalent based on our data.

Discussion. All of the participants in LeaderLab went through the same process in developing their action plans, so how might we account for the variation in the meaning the respondents assigned to the process? Several possibilities suggest themselves: (1) The program took a process perspective by having participants construct a plan in the first training week at CCL, implement the plan for three months back on the job, return to CCL and revise the action plan, and then implement again for two-and-a-half months back on the job. This process orientation was further enhanced by the relationship with the PA over the six months, which helped the participant reflect on what he or she was learning and revise actions accordingly. Thus, the program emphasizes a dynamic view of action planning. (2) Participants were encouraged to construct action plans which were meaningful and useful to them in their individual situation. (3) Participants typically had other leadership-development experiences which probably emphasized a more traditional goal-focus model of action planning. They may have carried this framework over into the program.

Although exploratory, this part of the study provides data on how action planning may work in actuality. These data challenge the way leadership and management-development professionals have typically viewed and presented action planning to their managerial/executive participants. It has most often been framed from the goal-attainment model, assuming that an action plan functions like a road map to get the participant from point A to point B. These data suggest that for many participants, action plans are much more dynamic. This preliminary finding is congruent with recent work by Mitchell and Wood (1994) who point out that, "Managerial work is characterized by complex causal paths, socially mediated outcomes, dynamic, evolving tasks, and multiple time frames. These characteristics make the application of goal-setting theory to managerial work more complex than simply setting specific, challenging goals" (p. 3).

Further studies are needed to explore more fully the models of action planning used by participants and the effectiveness of different models.

Implications

The implications of this study for effective action-taking relate primarily to practice, although we will mention a few research issues. With respect to practice, we see implications for three groups: program designers, potential participants, and program evaluators.

Practice

Program designers. This evaluation found that challenge, support, and opportunity are key ingredients in action-oriented leadership-development programs. Challenge can take many forms including feedback, experiential exercises (including nontraditional activities), relationships, and implementation of action plans in the leadership situation. Support can be provided through many different avenues such as relationships, learning journals, spreading learning over time, and practical content. Opportunities to experiment with changes and practice new actions are also important and can be built into the program during the training weeks as well as back in the leadership situation. The PA and change partners should be able to help the participant think through what might be appropriate opportunities for practice back home. What the PA and change partner relationships as well as the intervention stretched over six months may provide to the participant is *ongoing* support, challenge, and opportunities for experimentation and practice.

A major benefit of stretching the intervention over time is that participants are able to learn from their own actions through their experimentations and practice in their leadership situation. Patterns are repeated, unexpected situations arise that must be dealt with, and knowledge about actions taken can be accumulated. The opportunity to work within their own systems gives participants extra motivation to learn and improve effectiveness. The stakes are real when they attempt to try something new or alter existing patterns.

Supervisory involvement is widely advocated throughout the transfer-of-training literature (see Broad & Newstrom, 1992, for a thorough discussion). However, our study reveals that support can effectively come from outside the organization as well as inside it. There may be a unique value of relationships with outside coaches such as PAs. Participants may be freer to discuss any and all issues because there is no threat of repercussions. Also, the PA has access to a wealth of data (for example, journal data, 360-degree feedback, follow-up interviews) on the participant that organizational employees would not. Program designers may want to explore the value of these relationships in their own programs.

Using nontraditional training methods has several implications. First, there is value in using many different types of methods to break down barriers and gain new perspectives. Second, using innovative methods encourages risk-taking and experimentation to enhance learning. Also, these activities are congruent with the theme of doing or acting. They require participants to take action, not just think or feel. Our data also show that making decisions about programs and their methods based on participant ratings or reactions at one moment in time only may be a mistake. For example, the perceived value of artistic activities actually increased over time.

One final, but critical, point is that an action-oriented program must model what it is advocating. This means having a diverse staff if part of the program addresses diversity. It means including evaluation from the very beginning to continuously improve the program. This process helps the program staff learn from the actions they are taking, just as participants do. It also implies that data collection is built into the program to facilitate the continuous improvement and learning that needs to occur.

Potential participants. Who should attend action-oriented programs? Clearly it is for those who are serious about looking at themselves and their leadership situations with the intent to make change and take action. Participants must work over a period of time to reap the benefits. It would not be good for those who, for whatever reason, are unwilling or unable to work on themselves and their organizations. Even with support mechanisms built in, it takes time to use them, which requires commitment.

People who are experiencing a moderate amount of turbulence in their lives might find an action-oriented program very helpful. Those in very stable environments who are being extremely effective probably would not benefit because their motivation for change may be low. If the organizational context is chaotic, there may not be opportunities to use the program for changes and improvements. The program may be able to help participants, though, who are not very open to work on certain areas such as seeking feedback.

What can participants expect to get from such a program? The data show that participants who attend LeaderLab can expect that they will take more effective action (in many domains) in their leadership situation. This implication distinguishes it from many other leadership-development programs whose outcomes are primarily enhanced self-awareness or improvement in interpersonal skills. Although there was variety among the types of actions taken by participants, with few exceptions they were consistent in becoming more effective according to relevant others. Thus, participants who want to take action to improve their effectiveness could find an action-oriented program a useful vehicle through which to accomplish that goal.

Another important benefit is that participants both learn the value of developmental relationships and also gain skills in establishing these supportive relationships. They have opportunity to build meaningful relationships with others during the program, some of which they can continue after it is over.

Program evaluators. The existence of multiple models of action planning presents great difficulty for program evaluators. In fact, we believe that evaluators probably hold a particular model of action planning, and this may well influence the types of questions they ask. With the goal-focus model (see page 27), evaluators may only look at goals that were set in action planning or the program goal. This model is far easier to assess by simply checking off a yes or no for each action committed to on paper. The vision-focus and process-focus models are more dynamic and complex. In our own analysis strategy, we decided to forgo the typical goal-focus model of measuring progress. Thus, in our content analysis, we developed the list of *all* actions reported by at least two sources, rather than focusing only on what participants committed to on paper in the program. However, we could have gone further by looking at progress on the vision, for example.

We can educate ourselves and our clients by thinking through many of the possible questions we ask in program evaluations, rather than stopping at "Give me a number that says it worked or didn't work." Such limited investigation would probably miss much of the rich learning to be garnered from the evaluation; for instance, our exploratory questions on action planning revealed the turbulence present in the participants' lives.

We believe it is critical to not only examine outcomes but to frame our evaluations in ways that help us understand why the outcome was achieved or not achieved. As Noe and Ford (1992) point out, "We may know the outcome . . . but understand little about the more complex processes underlying this outcome" (p. 370). Program evaluation at CCL strives to add to our knowledge of the leadership development process and we are now focusing more on the methodologies involved in that process, as well as other factors.

Like others in the field we advocate a multimethod approach to evaluating leadership development programs. This is a very complex process to describe, document, and understand, and no one method can provide the rich information necessary. This may present difficulties for human-resources or training-and-development professionals who lack training in the area of program evaluation. One strategy is to involve others or form partnerships to gain the necessary expertise. We used an advisory group to help us deal with the complexities of this evaluation.[4] This worked well because we involved a variety of individuals who had different areas of expertise, including one of the PAs. The advisory group members also found it useful to brainstorm and think through ideas in a focused way with their colleagues. The group has met as needs have arisen. Involving others is an excellent strategy to improve the quality of the evaluation and to share learning within the organization.

Research

With respect to research, we see the following implications. Given the amount of turbulence we found in this study, it would appear the relationship between turbulence and actions taken by participants warrants further study. Both research and theory support the idea that moderately stressful situations can motivate people to take action to increase their effectiveness. Determining how turbulence facilitates program impact would be helpful to potential participants and their organizations in deciding whether the "timing is just right."

We also believe the findings related to different models of action planning can provide a rich research agenda for the future. If managers need models that are different from the traditional goal-attainment model, then our three models may provide a starting point for further exploration. The process that LeaderLab employs is dynamic and evolving, although it can only be taken so far within the six months of the program.

Reframing our thinking around action planning also has implications for the questions we ask about program effectiveness. The questions asked would probably depend upon which model is operant. Perhaps we should challenge ourselves to look beyond the goal-attainment model and think about questions on the evolution of action steps and visions.

Notes

1. This method helps eliminate measurement issues associated with the more traditional pre-post ratings; such issues include low intercorrelations among rater groups (McLean, Sytsma, & Kerwin-Ryberg, 1995) and response-shift bias (Howard & Dailey, 1979; Mezoff, 1991; Sprangers & Hoogstraten, 1989).

2. An explanation for the lack of significant differences on Sense of Purpose could be the result of selection bias. Since the control group was composed of future participants, it may be that people who apply and are accepted into LeaderLab are already engaged in working on their sense of purpose.

3. We should point out, however, that the differences between the two groups on Seeking Feedback were significant at the .08 level. Likewise, differences on Facilitating Communication were significant at the .08 level and differences on Climate were significant at the .03 level. Neither Climate nor Facilitating Communication are directly addressed by the program. Balancing work and personal life may be an ongoing issue for people in leadership roles, or it may be that raters are not able to assess this scale very well since they may not know firsthand the schedule kept by the participant. The mean change score for Balance based on the self-report data is almost twice the mean for the rater data but was still relatively low compared to the mean change on other scales.

4. These complexities engendered a number of limitations. Although our sample size is small, the results of this study should be generalizable to other LeaderLab participants. It is not clear whether these results would generalize to participants in other action-oriented leadership-development programs. Given the major contributions of process advisors and program structure, the results from LeaderLab may be most similar to programs which also include developmental relationships and extended interventions which integrate work and classroom training. Additional studies would be needed to determine if the results could be generalized.

Also, this study is not longitudinal. Data were collected, at most, five months post-program. So we don't know if the improvements in action taking are sustained over a longer period of time. Thus, we know that the program is meeting its goal in the short run, but we don't know if it works over the long term. This leaves two questions unanswered: "Is six months long enough for sustained changes in action?" and "Is the degree of intervention provided through LeaderLab enough to sustain changes in action over longer periods of time?" We hope to answer these in future studies.

We did not ask directly about turbulence in the interviews on action planning. Therefore our data are incomplete and should be viewed with caution. Also, different sources tended to provide different points of views in these interviews. For example, co-workers tended to provide more contextual information and PAs tended to provide more in-depth information on the individual's characteristics, style, and so on. Our data could have been enhanced by interviewing more than one co-worker to verify the contextual information. Unfortunately, there was no additional source to verify the PA information.

References

Argyris, C., Putnam, R., & Smith, D. (1985). *Action science.* San Francisco: Jossey-Bass.

Bandura, A. (1977). Self-efficacy: Toward a unifying theory of behavioral change. *Psychological Review, 84,* 191-215.

Bray, J. H., & Howard, G. S. (1980). Methodological considerations in the evaluation of a teacher-training program. *Journal of Educational Psychology, 72*(1), 62-70.

Broad, M. L., & Newstrom, J. W. (1992). *Transfer of training: Action-packed strategies to ensure high payoff from training investments.* Reading, MA: Addison-Wesley.

Bunker, K. A., & Webb, A. D. (1992). *Learning how to learn from experience: Impact of stress and coping.* Greensboro, NC: Center for Creative Leadership.

Burnside, R. M., & Guthrie, V. A. (1992). *Training for action: A new approach to executive development.* Greensboro, NC: Center for Creative Leadership.

Cell, E. (1984). *Learning to learn from experience.* Albany: State University of New York.

Cohen, J. (1988). *Statistical power analysis for the behavioral sciences* (2nd ed.). Hillsdale, NJ: Erlbaum.

Conger, J. A. (1992). *Learning to lead: The art of transforming managers into leaders.* San Francisco: Jossey-Bass.

De Ciantis, C. (1995). *Using an art technique to facilitate leadership development.* Greensboro, NC: Center for Creative Leadership.

Dixon, N. M. (1994). *The organizational learning cycle: How we can learn collectively.* New York: McGraw-Hill.

Glass, G. V., & Hopkins, K. D. (1984). *Statistical methods in education and psychology* (2nd ed.). Englewood Cliffs, NJ: Prentice Hall.

Hoogstraten, J. (1982). The retrospective pretest in an educational training context. *Journal of Experimental Education, 50*(4), 200-204.

Howard, G. S., & Dailey, P. R. (1979). Response-shift bias: A source of contamination of self-report measures. *Journal of Applied Psychology, 64*(2), 144-150.

Howard, G. S., Ralph, K. M., Gulanick, N. A., Maxwell, S. E., Nance, D. W., & Gerber, S. K. (1979, Winter). Internal invalidity in pretest-posttest self-report evaluation and re-evaluations of retrospective pretests. *Applied Psychological Measurement, 3*(1), 1-123.

Kram, K. E. (1988). *Mentoring at work: Developmental relationships in organizational life.* Lanham, MD: University Press of America.

McCall, M. W., Jr., Lombardo, M. M., & Morrison, A. M. (1988). *The lessons of experience: How successful executives develop on the job.* Lexington, MA: Lexington Books.

McCauley, C. D., & Hughes-James, M. W. (1994). *An evaluation of the outcomes of a leadership development program.* Greensboro, NC: Center for Creative Leadership.

McCauley, C. D., & Young, D. P. (1993). Creating developmental relationships: Roles and strategies. *Human Resource Management Review, 3*(3), 219-230.

McLean, G. N., Sytsma, M. R., & Kerwin-Ryberg, K. (1995, March). *Using 360-degree feedback to evaluate management development: New data, new insights.* Paper presented at the Annual Conference of the Academy of Human Resources Development, St. Louis.

Mezoff, B. (1991, September). How to get accurate self-reports of training outcomes. *Training and Development Journal, 35*(9), 57-61.

Mitchell, T. R., & Wood, R. E. (1994). Managerial goal setting. *Journal of Leadership Studies, 1*(2), 3-26.

Morrison, A. M. (1992). *The new leaders: Guidelines on leadership diversity in America.* San Francisco: Jossey-Bass.

Noe, R. A., & Ford, J. K. (1992). Emerging issues and new directions for training research. *Research in Personnel and Human Resources Management, 10,* 345-384.

Noel, J. L., & Charan, R. (1989). Leadership development at GE's Crotonville. In A. A. Vicere (Ed.), *Executive education: Process, practice, and evaluation* (pp. 205-218). Princeton, NJ: Peterson's Guides.

Petranek, C. F., Corey, S., & Black, R. (1992). Three levels of learning in simulations: Participating, debriefing, and journal writing. *Simulation and Gaming, 23*(2), 174-185.

Pohl, N. F. (1982). Using retrospective pre-ratings to counteract response-shift confounding. *Journal of Experimental Education, 50*(4), 211-214.

Revans, R. (1983). *ABC of action learning.* Bromley, Kent, England: Chartwell-Bratt Ltd.

Richards, D. (1995). *Artful work: Awakening joy, meaning, and commitment in the workplace.* San Francisco: Berrett-Koehler.

Sadler, P. (1989). Educating managers for the twenty-first century. In A. A. Vicere (Ed.), *Executive education: Process, practice, and evaluation* (pp. 43-62). Princeton, NJ: Peterson's Guides.

Sprangers, M., & Hoogstraten, J. (1989). Pretesting effects in retrospective pretest-posttest designs. *Journal of Applied Psychology, 74*(2), 265-272.

Vaill, P. B. (1989). *Managing as a performing art: New ideas for a world of chaotic change.* San Francisco: Jossey-Bass.

Wills, S. (1994). 2001: A research odyssey. *Journal of Management Development, 13*(1). Bradford, West Yorkshire, England: MCB University Press.

Yerkes, R., & Dodson, J. D. (1908). The relationship of stimulus to rapidity of habit formation. *Journal of Comparative Neurological Psychology, 18.*

Young, D. P. (1993, April). *Using evaluation to build leadership development programs.* Paper presented at the Assessment, Measurement and Evaluation Conference, Santa Clara, CA.

Young, D. P., & Burnside, R. M. (1993, March 29). *LeaderLab: Future, present, past.* Colloquium at the Center for Creative Leadership.

Young, D. P., & Hefferan, J. (1994). *LeaderLab® program feedback report.* Unpublished manuscript, Center for Creative Leadership, Greensboro, NC.

Appendix: Further Information on Outcome Studies

Table A1: Alphas for *Impact Questionnaire*

Category Name	Alpha Year Ago N = 106	Alpha Now N = 106	Alpha Difference Scores N = 106
Competencies:			
Coping with Emotional Disequilibrium	.87	.85	.66
Interpersonal Relationships	.93	.92	.88
Flexibility	.80	.78	.55
Organizational Systems	.81	.78	.65
Trade-offs	.86	.86	.67
Other:			
Balance	.17	.78	.79
Climate	.70	.58	.57
Facilitating Communication	.80	.83	.74
Seeking Feedback	.83	.80	.73
Listening	.84	.80	.78
Self-assessment	.85	.82	.76
Self-confidence	.61	.56	.63
Sense of Purpose	.54	.60	.40
Subordinate Development	.85	.84	.76

Note: Raw scores were used to compute the alpha.

Note: The above alphas were computed for the *Now* ratings, *Year Ago* ratings, and the *Difference* scores between *Now* and *Year Ago*. It should be noted that the alpha for Balance using the *Year Ago* ratings was extremely low (.17), although the *Now* ratings and *Difference* ratings are acceptable (.78 and .79, respectively). Also worth noting is the low alpha for the Sense of Purpose category using the *Difference* ratings (.40). We had difficulty constructing items for this category and this shows in its low alphas.

Data from First Set of Telephone Interviews—
Categories and Definitions for Actions Taken

*Competencies**

Coping with Emotional Disequilibrium—remaining calm and level-headed in the face of events that alter one's emotions, even to high levels of arousal.

Interpersonal Relationships—involves the manner in which individuals *relate* to others interpersonally in both work and social contexts (in non-instrumental ways).

Organizational Systems—changes in organizational practices that may affect only a specific group or the entire organization.

Other

Balance/Family—devoting more time to family/leisure activities and less to work-related tasks or issues.

Health—changes in way participants attend to their physical/mental health such as exercising, eating habits, meditating, etc.

Climate—altering a workgroup's or organization's psychological environment.

Communication/Listening—changes in the way an individual sends, receives, and processes information to and from other individuals or groups.

Feedback—changes in the amount of, the type of, or the manner of collecting critical information received from others about the self.

Organizing the Job/Work—organizing and prioritizing tasks and issues faced on the job.

Openness—increasing the amount of self-disclosure; emotional accessibility; open-mindedness to the ideas of others.

Perspective Taking—looking at issues and situations using various points of view.

Self-awareness/Reflection—sensitivity to, introspection of, and evaluation of actions and thoughts regarding the self, resulting in revised self-image.

Self-confidence—having assurance or certainty about oneself or one's abilities.

Sense of Purpose/Vision—forming and pursuing an ideal future state that guides one's actions.

Subordinate Development—providing important opportunities to subordinates and/or enhancing their careers. Includes increased delegation, empowerment, etc.

Roles—changes by the participant regarding the role(s) he or she plays at work. May involve redefinition of roles, taking on new roles, or dropping roles.

Getting Resources—obtaining necessary resources (dollars, people, etc.) to support group's mission.

Utilizing LeaderLab Content or Processes—sharing or employing the LeaderLab materials/processes back in the workplace.

Career—exploration or changes made in career/job/leadership situation.

Miscellaneous

*Two of the five competencies (Flexibility and Trade-offs) were not major themes in the data.

Further Details on Outcome Studies

Our first analysis used only the data of participants who completed the program, to determine if they had made significant changes in actions taken (see Table 4, page 14). We first computed mean difference scores using rater data only for each category. (*Year Ago Average* was subtracted from *Now Average* because we assumed participants would generally have higher scores *Now*.) We then computed paired *t*-tests for each to determine if the differences were significantly greater than zero by chance alone. In order to account for the increased potential of Type I errors due to multiple *t*-tests, we adjusted our significance level to .01 instead of .05.

The group that completed the program was perceived as having made significant, positive change in every category by their raters except Balance. The greatest perceived change was on Self-assessment ($t = 8.52$, $p = .0001$) and the smallest perceived change was on Balance ($t = 1.63$, $p = .11$).

Next, we computed mean difference scores (again using only rater data) for the control group. We then computed *t*-tests for independent samples comparing the difference scores of the control group with the group that completed LeaderLab. Again, we used .01 as our significance level, not .05.

Significance testing should not be used to indicate the magnitude of the difference—instead, effect size should be computed and reported (Glass & Hopkins, 1984). We have computed *d* using the formula for independent samples with unequal standard deviations (Cohen, 1988, p. 67) for each scale—the results are shown in Table A2. The effect sizes ranged from .25 to .55. Cohen (1988, pp. 25-27) has characterized effect sizes as follows: .2 is small; .5 is moderate; and .8 is large. Our results indicate that four categories have smaller effect sizes ranging from .25 to .38 (Sense of Purpose, Seeking Feedback, Facilitating Communication, and Balance). The others have more moderate effect sizes ranging from .4 to .55. Scales with *d*s of .40 or higher are Interpersonal Relationships, Coping with Emotional Disequilibrium, Trade-offs, Self-assessment, Flexibility, Organizational Systems, Climate, Subordinate Development, Listening, and Self-confidence. It is worth noting that Self-assessment had the lowest mean score based on the *Year Ago* ratings (refer to Table 4, page 14), so there was much room for improvement in this domain in the eyes of the raters.

We also analyzed the impact-on-effectiveness ratings to see if, in fact, the changes made by participants were perceived by others as resulting in increased effectiveness. We used only the rater data for the participant group in this analysis. We computed simple correlations between the mean difference scores by item and the impact-on-effectiveness ratings. For 83 of the 92 items Pearson's *r* was positive and .3 or higher. The highest *r* was .88. On 9

Table A2
Effect Size

Category	Mean Change Group That Completed LeaderLab (N = 29)	Mean Change Control Group (N = 38)	d
Competencies:			
Flexibility	.63	.34	.46
Organizational Systems	.63	.35	.46
Interpersonal Relationships	.62	.27	.55
Coping with Emotional Disequilibrium	.52	.21	.55
Trade-offs	.51	.25	.54
Other:			
Self-assessment	.92	.44	.53
Seeking Feedback	.77	.50	.29
Climate	.59	.28	.42
Facilitating Communication	.57	.35	.32
Subordinate Development	.55	.32	.40
Listening	.50	.22	.49
Sense of Purpose	.32	.21	.26
Self-confidence	.22	.08	.42
Balance	.20	.02	.25

items Pearson's *r* was below .3 and on one item there was a small negative correlation. Overall, these results indicate that if participants got higher ratings *Now* (versus a *Year Ago*) on the item, they were seen as being more effective. Conversely, if participants got lower ratings *Now* than a *Year Ago* on the item, they were seen as being less effective.

There are two areas in which the data should be approached with caution. There could be an inflation effect of the post-then retrospective methodology. This is still a relatively new method for program evaluations and there may be effects that we are unaware of. However, several studies have suggested that most training impact is underestimated using the pre-post methodology, and that the post-then retrospective method more accurately reflects training impact (Bray & Howard, 1980; Hoogstraten, 1982; Howard & Dailey, 1979; Howard, Ralph, Gulanick, Maxwell, Nance, & Gerber, 1979; Pohl, 1982). Second, we encouraged participants to use change partners as part of their rater group. Given that change partners are very aware of the changes participants are attempting and that part of their role is to provide support for those changes, they may have responded more favorably to the participants' attempts to take more effective action.

Index

CENTER FOR CREATIVE LEADERSHIP PUBLICATIONS

SELECTED REPORTS:

The Adventures of Team Fantastic: A Practical Guide for Team Leaders and Members
G.L. Hallam (1996, Stock #172) $20.00

Beyond Work-Family Programs J.R. Kofodimos (1995, Stock #167) $25.00

CEO Selection: A Street-smart Review G.P. Hollenbeck (1994, Stock #164) $25.00

Coping With an Intolerable Boss M.M. Lombardo & M.W. McCall, Jr. (1984, Stock #305) $10.00

The Creative Opportunists: Conversations with the CEOs of Small Businesses
J.S. Bruce (1992, Stock #316) $12.00

Creativity in the R&D Laboratory T.M. Amabile & S.S. Gryskiewicz (1987, Stock #130) $12.00

The Dynamics of Management Derailment M.M. Lombardo & C.D. McCauley (1988, Stock #134). $12.00

Eighty-eight Assignments for Development in Place: Enhancing the Developmental
Challenge of Existing Jobs M.M. Lombardo & R.W. Eichinger (1989, Stock #136) $15.00

Enhancing 360-degree Feedback for Senior Executives: How to Maximize the Benefits and
Minimize the Risks R.E. Kaplan & C.J. Palus (1994, Stock #160) $15.00

An Evaluation of the Outcomes of a Leadership Development Program C.D. McCauley &
M.W. Hughes-James (1994, Stock #163) $35.00

Evolving Leaders: A Model for Promoting Leadership Development in Programs C.J. Palus &
W.H. Drath (1995, Stock #165) $20.00

Feedback to Managers, Volume I: A Guide to Evaluating Multi-rater Feedback Instruments
E. Van Velsor & J. Brittain Leslie (1991, Stock #149) $20.00

Feedback to Managers, Volume II: A Review and Comparison of Sixteen Multi-rater
Feedback Instruments E. Van Velsor & J. Brittain Leslie (1991, Stock #150) $80.00

Forceful Leadership and Enabling Leadership: You Can Do Both R.E. Kaplan (1996, Stock #171) $20.00

Gender Differences in the Development of Managers: How Women Managers Learn From
Experience E. Van Velsor & M. W. Hughes (1990, Stock #145) $35.00

A Glass Ceiling Survey: Benchmarking Barriers and Practices A.M. Morrison, C.T. Schreiber,
& K.F. Price (1995, Stock #161) $20.00

Helping Leaders Take Effective Action: A Program Evaluation D.P. Young & N.M. Dixon
(1996, Stock #174) $18.00

How to Design an Effective System for Developing Managers and Executives M.A. Dalton &
G.P. Hollenbeck (1996, Stock #158) $15.00

The Intuitive Pragmatists: Conversations with Chief Executive Officers J.S. Bruce
(1986, Stock #310) $12.00

Key Events in Executives' Lives E.H. Lindsey, V. Homes, & M.W. McCall, Jr.
(1987, Stock #132) $65.00

Leadership for Turbulent Times L.R. Sayles (1995, Stock #325) $20.00

Learning How to Learn From Experience: Impact of Stress and Coping K.A. Bunker &
A.D. Webb (1992, Stock #154) $30.00

A Look at Derailment Today: North America and Europe J. Brittain Leslie & E. Van Velsor
(1996, Stock #169) $25.00

Making Common Sense: Leadership as Meaning-making in a Community of Practice
W.H. Drath & C.J. Palus (1994, Stock #156) $15.00

Managerial Promotion: The Dynamics for Men and Women M.N. Ruderman, P.J. Ohlott, &
K.E. Kram (1996, Stock #170) $15.00

Managing Across Cultures: A Learning Framework M.S. Wilson, M.H. Hoppe, & L.R. Sayles
(1996, Stock #173) $15.00

Off the Track: Why and How Successful Executives Get Derailed M.W. McCall, Jr., &
M.M. Lombardo (1983, Stock #121) $10.00

Perspectives on Dialogue: Making Talk Developmental for Individuals and Organizations
N.M. Dixon (1996, Stock #168) $20.00

Preventing Derailment: What To Do Before It's Too Late M.M. Lombardo &
R.W. Eichinger (1989, Stock #138) $25.00

The Realities of Management Promotion M.N. Ruderman & P.J. Ohlott (1994, Stock #157) $20.00

Redefining What's Essential to Business Performance: Pathways to Productivity,
Quality, and Service L.R. Sayles (1990, Stock #142) $20.00

Succession Planning: An Annotated Bibliography L.J. Eastman (1995, Stock #324) $20.00

Training for Action: A New Approach to Executive Development R.M. Burnside &
V.A. Guthrie (1992, Stock #153) $15.00

Traps and Pitfalls in the Judgment of Executive Potential M.N. Ruderman & P.J. Ohlott
(1990, Stock #141) $20.00

Twenty-two Ways to Develop Leadership in Staff Managers R.W. Eichinger & M.M. Lombardo (1990, Stock #144) $15.00

Upward-communication Programs in American Industry A.I. Kraut & F.H. Freeman (1992, Stock #152) $30.00

Using an Art Technique to Facilitate Leadership Development C. De Ciantis (1995, Stock #166)... $30.00

Why Executives Lose Their Balance J.R. Kofodimos (1989, Stock #137) $20.00

Why Managers Have Trouble Empowering: A Theoretical Perspective Based on Concepts of Adult Development W.H. Drath (1993, Stock #155) $15.00

SELECTED BOOKS:

Balancing Act: How Managers Can Integrate Successful Careers and Fulfilling Personal Lives J.R. Kofodimos (1993, Stock #247) $27.00

Beyond Ambition: How Driven Managers Can Lead Better and Live Better R.E. Kaplan, W.H. Drath, & J.R. Kofodimos (1991, Stock #227) $29.95

Breaking the Glass Ceiling: Can Women Reach the Top of America's Largest Corporations? (Updated Edition) A.M. Morrison, R.P. White, & E. Van Velsor (1992, Stock #236A) $13.00

Choosing to Lead (Second Edition) K.E. Clark & M.B. Clark (1996, Stock #327) $25.00

Developing Diversity in Organizations: A Digest of Selected Literature A.M. Morrison & K.M. Crabtree (1992, Stock #317) $25.00

Discovering Creativity: Proceedings of the 1992 International Creativity and Innovation Networking Conference S.S. Gryskiewicz (Ed.) (1993, Stock #319) $30.00

Executive Selection: A Look at What We Know and What We Need to Know D.L. DeVries (1993, Stock #321) $20.00

Healing the Wounds: Overcoming the Trauma of Layoffs and Revitalizing Downsized Organizations D.M. Noer (1993, Stock #245) $27.50

If I'm In Charge Here, Why Is Everybody Laughing? D.P. Campbell (1984, Stock #205) $8.95

If You Don't Know Where You're Going You'll Probably End Up Somewhere Else D.P. Campbell (1974, Stock #203) $9.40

Inklings: Collected Columns on Leadership and Creativity D.P. Campbell (1992, Stock #233) $15.00

Leadership Education 1996-1997: A Source Book (Sixth Edition), Vol. 1, Courses and Programs F.H. Freeman, K.B. Knott, & M.K. Schwartz (Eds.) (1996, Stock #330) $35.00

Leadership Education 1996-1997: A Source Book (Sixth Edition), Vol. 2, Leadership Resources F.H. Freeman, K.B. Knott, & M.K. Schwartz (Eds.) (1996, Stock #331) $35.00

Leadership: Enhancing the Lessons of Experience (Second Edition) R.L. Hughes, R.C. Ginnett, & G.J. Curphy (1996, Stock #266) $49.95

The Lessons of Experience: How Successful Executives Develop on the Job M.W. McCall, Jr., M.M. Lombardo, & A.M. Morrison (1988, Stock #211) $22.95

Making Diversity Happen: Controversies and Solutions A.M. Morrison, M.N. Ruderman, & M. Hughes-James (1993, Stock #320) $25.00

The New Leaders: Guidelines on Leadership Diversity in America A.M. Morrison (1992, Stock #238) $29.00

Readings in Innovation S.S. Gryskiewicz & D.A. Hills (Eds.) (1992, Stock #240) $25.00

Selected Research on Work Team Diversity M.N. Ruderman, M.W. Hughes-James, & S.E. Jackson (Eds.) (1996, Stock #326) $24.95

Take the Road to Creativity and Get Off Your Dead End D.P. Campbell (1977, Stock #204) $8.95

Whatever It Takes: The Realities of Managerial Decision Making (Second Edition) M.W. McCall, Jr., & R.E. Kaplan (1990, Stock #218) $30.40

The Working Leader: The Triumph of High Performance Over Conventional Management Principles L.R. Sayles (1993, Stock #243) $24.95

SPECIAL PACKAGES:

Conversations with CEOs (includes 310 & 316) $16.00

Development & Derailment (includes 136, 138, & 144) $25.00

The Diversity Collection (includes 145, 236, 238, 317, & 320) $85.00

Executive Selection Package (includes 141, 321, & 157) $32.00

Feedback to Managers—Volumes I & II (includes 149 & 150) $85.00

Personal Growth, Taking Charge, and Enhancing Creativity (includes 203, 204, & 205) $20.00

Leadership Education 1996-1997: A Source Book—Volumes 1 & 2 (includes 330 & 331) $60.00

Discounts are available. Please write for a comprehensive Publications catalog. Address your request to: Publication, Center for Creative Leadership, P.O. Box 26300, Greensboro, NC 27438-6300, 910-545-2805, or fax to 910-545-3221. All prices subject to change.